In the Awakening Season

In the Awakening Season

Poems

Matthew Mumber

LEAPFOLIO
A JOINT-VENTURE PARTNER OF TUPELO PRESS
NORTH ADAMS, MASSACHUSETTS

Library of Congress Cataloging-in-Publication data available upon request

ISBN: 978-1-946507-06-8

Cover and text designed by adam b. bohannon

Cover art: *Winter prune, Spring bloom,* by Matthew Mumber.

First edition: September 2020.

Leapfolio, a joint-venture partner of Tupelo Press
P.O. Box 1767, North Adams, Massachusetts 01247
(413) 664–9611 / info@leapfolio.net / www.leapfolio.net
www.tupelopress.org

—for my patients

contents

For once on the face of the earth,
let's not speak in any language;
let's stop for one second,
and not move our arms so much...

...Perhaps the earth can teach us
as when everything seems dead
and later proves to be alive.

"KEEPING QUIET"
PABLO NERUDA

Praised be your name, no one.
For your sake
we shall flower.
Towards
you.
A nothing
we were, are, shall
remain, flowering.

"PSALM"
PAUL CELAN

:awaken:

First Flowering

In winter surround,
       flouting perils of future frost,
a backyard Japanese cherry
     heralds spring
     with impossible pink fluorescence.

     I feel like a prophet,
     unwelcome
     in my hometown,
     speaking of springs unseen—
always ahead of Times.

Connected

—*Day two of a five-day, silent retreat with Thich Nhat Hanh*

Mid-morning, after dawn meditation,
Thay tells us,
Go for a mindful walk,
enjoy nature.

Most others walk
then sit near him—
our revered teacher.

I settle into a corner of an open field,
grass sleeping, mid-fall.
The mottled sunlight
highlights
a single autumn leaf
quaking and turning and
rising and falling with
an imperceptible wind,
somehow suspended, eye level,
mid-air, just to the side of me,
a maple tree branch above, leaf-strewn earth below.
My closer inspection reveals
an invisible spider thread
thinly attached to the stem.

Mesmerized,
I sit until the distant bell calls me back.

The next day
after morning meditation,
the whole group files out,
mindfully walking along

a different dirt path in the woods;
just above their heads
I see
a single leaf suspended.

On Being a Doctor

The family invited me
to a small, tree-planting memorial
where I half-cried my way through
a poem written
for this patient,
a group member who just died,

who outlived expectations,
made new friends in the process,
fought to the very end,
peacefully released.

Afterwards
her son-in-law
tried to console me.

I remember mostly
the half-dozen goldfinches
happily upside down and
sideways, clinging
to suet cages, eating,
not noticing us at all.

Breaking News

Every day, right at your fingertips: the circus. Giant
sharks, mom kills child while shopping, spider

throws snake, bikini celebrities, DUI, albino alligators.
Just click right here for the crap-tastic, and then

the real show begins. We call it news, and its really
just advertising, selling the opinions of the highest payer.

'Cause they know who's out to kill you, steal
your guns and money, they know who you need

to fear and worship with your voice (and votes). Why
drop flyers from the sky when they can come and sit

at your dinner table, quiet and private like,
just a little nudge here and there to help

you understand the top 5 things to binge,
consume, deny, plan, engage, discuss, forget.

They water the seeds, though you still get to
choose which ones

for now.

Commencement

For Katelyn

Fifteen thousand years after glaciers
chiseled out our valley, today,
your graduation day,
this football stadium stands empty
as a single strand of RNA pulls the plug
on your prom pictures, makes this space
where Class of 2020 photos cycle,
Jumbotrons fall silent in steady procession.
Your face has its 15 seconds, and something proud
inside stands up, gets goose bumps, the earth trembles.
The day quiets, sits down, watches
the thousand beginnings of everything
we have names for, listens for the slow grind
of ice against bedrock.

:awaken:

Cancer Walk

I let a daisy drop
into the brown river,
watch as it floats
toward the banks of the levy,
the broken dam,
to sea,

a single, stemmed daisy—
green, white, yellow—
weightless,
particular

from seed to first bloom,
like you here—
boundless.

Sermon on the Hill

Today,
a dream comes
in that slowed-down space
between sleep
and wide awake,
where seconds are minutes
and minutes hours.

Midday
I am standing unnoticed by the Capitol building
in Washington DC, on a grassy area
just outside of a black metal fence,
with others entrenched
in their individual pursuits:

a security guard looking mechanically
at nothing in particular,

a young mother
pushing her sleeping child in a blue-and-white, covered stroller,

a couple of men with gray-green veterans hats,
pointing this way and that,
examining a tri-fold laminated map.

Something wells up,
as though some unseen signal tunes in
to an AM radio channel
in my mind, and I speak out loud.

Blessed are those who offer iron-fist protection to the insecure.
The cold comfort of their graves will be like a finely leathered living room.

Blessed are those who succeed solely on their own merits.

       The commodity of celebrity will promote and protect their brand.

Blessed are those who live in steel certainty.

       They will never be wrong.

Blessed are those who eternally defend, attack, and deny.

       They shall escape persecution in their own name's sake.

All around my knees and legs
there is what appears to be a broken mirror
about the size of my own torso,
split into tens of pieces.
I begin to piece the shards together
like a puzzle with linear spaces
between parts.

The older veteran gives me a piece of cardboard
from the side of the road
that looks like the roof of a makeshift shanty.
The young mother offers some glue.
Sliver by shard
I arrange the mirror mosaic
then hang it from my neck,
over my chest,
facing outward,
using handcuffs
from the security guard.

I stand,
begin walking around the outdoor mall.

A passerby, vaguely familiar, glances in my direction:

Blessed are those who are broken,
　　　　for they shall be made whole.

In a flash of light,

I awaken.

Resurrection

Here, in this moment
where our skin is submerged,
and there are no shrouds,
no reputations
to unravel,
die with me
just once
while we are still breathing,

only holding
       the greatest possible good,
       complete and utter despair,
       without preference—
to
die,
wake,
taste
this exquisite life.

Can we stop
everything together,
notice
that the flow of breath
continues
without our willing it so?

Liminal

At the dining-room table,
in a firm-backed chair,
feet flat on the floor:
roots sprout
from my toes,
sink deep toward earth's core,
an invisible thread
aligning spine
from the crown of my head
skyward.

I wait here unformed,
longing,
between
unknown
and known,
a space,
pregnant,
quivering.

If Medicine Were My Spouse

If medicine were my spouse
I would ask politely
if we could have a long-overdue chat.

I would arrange
a particular place and time
where we would not be bothered.

There would be abundant quiet
and fresh spring flowers.

We would begin
by giving each other thanks,
then I would pause,
breathing in and out,
and the flower petals would flutter slightly
with each exhale
and then be still.

Then I would speak slowly
about the grief unprocessed over
bad patient outcomes,
shame from teachers
for not knowing everything,
the guilt of not being able to fix it all
for everyone
and still getting paid,
the feelings of insecurity, inadequacy,
as though perfection
were possible,
self-neglect and doubt fueling
relentless pursuit

of limitless knowledge,
avoidance of certain failure.

The flower petals would move
and then be still for a very long while,
the sweet scent of daffodils
mixed in with the open flesh smell
of healing by secondary intention.

On the Day of Departure

No symphonies swell,
no curtains part.
Bells do not relentlessly ring—
just one step following another.

The packing and unpacking of things:
rolled-up underwear, paired socks, shirts,
solid-colored towels, new blue sheets,
a mini refrigerator and microwave,
packages of rainbow-flavored gummy worms.

Logistics rule attention:
registration,
orientation,
superficial greetings
and official reassurances.

A final hug:
18 years of nurturance
simply and necessarily
cut off with surgical precision.

Unable to sleep, I pray,
mind wandering deep
into the clouded unknown.
I feel separation,
lack of control,
loss of personal significance.
I fear
the known difficulties

of embodied human life,
certain death,

all punctuated
by labor spasms,
the first newborn cry
a parting song.

I ask to feel
what God feels
in relation to each
individual for eternity,

letting go
one by one by one—
each born upside down
and naked.

Contagion

I don't miss it all, spring training,
the 20 minutes per day, minimum,
spent checking on the Giants
box score, standings, reading that
Posey should bat second
or Panda's career is over—
I a fan for 40 years, several
World Series Championship hats
in possession.

Today the spring air feels silky smooth.
The cardboard plant no longer
billows its own atmosphere
across the county.
Stadiums stand empty
like the Roman Coliseum
without tourists,
hospitals half full except
for patients on ventilators
starving for breath.

Last night, I was awakened.
At 2 a.m., a mockingbird
chirped a hundred different songs
just outside my bedroom
window, no doubt inspired
by a clearly visible full moon,
exactly overhead.

Destiny

Breathe with me,
        this ordinary day,
leaf-lined dirt path, downhill,
        right next to home.

Take one step
        then another, without direction,
who knows if we will ever
        find our way back.

Just imagine if
        each second had a reason
        every created thing played its part
        nothing was ever wasted.

Even those missteps
that twist our limbs,
        roots of forgiveness.

Imagine each and every step
        a great allowing.

:falling:

From 32,000 Feet

The light of the sun
is alive,
conscious,
sees us all as rocks.

Someday
we will let loose
this cumbersome carbon,
join shining.

:falling:

Student of a Groundless Fall

People who teach people
to jump
out of perfectly good airplanes
say the only part that still
scares them is the landing,
where fall meets firmness.

Not that adventurous,
I book the standard flight
to enlightenment,
sit, spine straightened skyward,
gravity pinning pelvis to ground.
I clear departure,
achieve proper altitude
above the usual catastrophes,
notice
here and *now* have an edge:

slightest sensation,
most intimate thought,
this single breath
free-falling awake
forever.

:falling:

Limitless Participation

On the north-facing porch this morning,
two dogs snore;
a charcoal-gray cat scans.

A couple of black flies
and a tiny tan moth
frame the hazy humid valley below.

After last night's thunderstorm,
only the highest, wispy tree branches
sway—
just a little.

Air handlers rumble
along with invisible airplanes above
cars below
the occasional piercing chirp of a mockingbird.

I arrive in this present,
home.

:falling:

Dilemma

My son wants to play
college basketball. I don't
know how to support him.

He has loved it since
he was a boy, and is good
at it. He can jump,

shoot, pass, dribble up
and down the court, dunk and
hit the three. He's fast

works hard, great teammate,
and, oh yeah, he is 6 foot
seven and a half feet tall and ripped.

Smart too, brings his team
GPA up, wants to go
into medicine.

Had a blood clot, could
have killed him, right around time
to be recruited

in high school. Took out
his first rib, we still have it
in formalin inside a sealed plastic jar.

Chose a D1 school
as a preferred walk-on and
redshirted first year.

:falling:

Coach said there is an
opportunity
to play here for you.

Coach lied. He plays just kids
whose coaches he has to appease
so they will stay and

more from their home
program will feed into his
team in the future.

So hard to see him
sit on the bench, watching
others with equal

skills get a chance, while
he can only cheer them on,
play hard in practice.

I catch myself, at
times, rooting for the other
team, or for his team

to do worse, so that
he will get a chance, other
than in garbage time.

Afterwards, I hug
him and tell him that I love
him and am very

:falling:

proud. Keep working hard.
It will pay off in time, and
you will get your chance.

But then, I wake up
at 3 a.m. and wonder.

:falling:

On Being a Parent

I long for the days of dirty diapers—
days more like mowing the lawn,
unkempt,
then beautifully landscaped,
addressed,
cleaned,
finished for now.

I watch my children
learn life the hard way,
fail to be the best player,
student, participant.
I observe as they
interact in groups
when they don't know I'm looking.

I wish I could snap my fingers,
make it all fair.

In the middle of the night
when the phone rings,
I want to be strong enough
to stay on the line.

:falling:

Love Letter

It's complicated,
I know.
It's made that way.
It's like
a 6th-grade school yard at recess.

There's the grass, dirt,
balls,
and the bullies,
the popular kids,
and the loners
on the outskirts,
teachers looking the other way,
ongoing traffic,
sky

an ever-evolving
jigsaw puzzle,
never a wrong piece.
What is unreal
just doesn't fit,
and is nothing at all.

I am in the center
of everything.

:falling:

Fine Tuning

Sitting still
I sense
freedom
in the tiniest of things.

Usually
I feel free
buying supplements online,
throwing a Frisbee
with Teddy, my Border Collie.

Right here
there is light
specks of dust mid-air,
floating random.

I hardly ever notice
what is always
already present.

Kindness Returned

I watch and listen to the birds.

On slow days,
I talk out loud
and wonder if they listen,
as they chirp, flutter, preen
and wait for me to leave.

Once a week,
twice in deep winter,
I fill up two plastic 32-ounce gas station cups,
and one half that size,
with black sunflower seeds,
then dutifully march them over
to fill the forest green cylindrical feeder
found at a yard sale a few years ago
for two dollars (best bargain ever).

Every spring
some random soil
issues forth a medium-sized, spiky sun.

The birds seem to watch
as I am fed by these,
favorites of all flowers.

:falling:

Red Wasp

I unstack the brown plastic
Adirondack chairs, sit
then cry out,
deep asking,
Help me
forgive,
this full-moon morning,
still dark:

aching groan,
sweet silence.

Suddenly,
a hot-barb sting, left groin.
I jump up, strip naked,
red wasp flickering on the stone deck.

I smash it hard
with my right-foot flip-flop,
crush a few times,
go back to the house
for wound care.

First light now
         there they are
several wasps crawling around, homeless,
circling a small, paper-holed nest.

Calm now,
I spray the poison,

:falling:

watch them die,
wipe the chair dry,

sit.

:falling:

Jealousy

Is the daffodil envious
of the oak tree slumber

in spring? Does the oak
desire the daffodil's scent

and color? What about
one daffodil relative

to another? Better soil, more
leaves, ruffles? Does the flower fear

comparison,
that it will be found

somehow lacking
through some fault of its own?

:falling:

I Don't Know How to Pray

I don't know how to pray,
despite years of practice,
learned teachers and methods.

questioning,
listening,
watching,
longing,
asking nothing easy,

clinging and resisting to
thoughts, intentions, worries,
a sudden itch
punctuated by
occasional blissful silence—

deep within
poverty of efforts,
an unplanned meeting
with a love
whose intention to be with me
has equal foundation
in not knowing exactly how.

:falling:

Sleepwalking

If I ever get bored
with the river rapids' roar,
promise
you'll give me a nudge.

If I ever seem rushed
in our morning first touch,
hold me,
in a little longer hug.

When I start to forget
the gift of every breath,
promise
you'll be there to wake me.

:falling:

Sweat

I feel cold,
wind-bitten,
throwing a cloth Frisbee
with Teddy.

It's the type of cold that burns.
Even with that, I am able to sweat,
sweating a talent and a curse
passed down from my father.

Comfortable sweat.
Happy sweat.
Embarrassed sweat.
Hurried, focused, purified sweat.

Not-too-helpful sweat
when I was a waiter
and a customer asked,
Are you alright? or in surgery

when my hair-mask was soaked:
Don't drip on the surgical field, son.

A friend, whose specialty is reframing,
called it the mark of a true athlete,
physical efficiency.

After 54 years,
I am finally coming to befriend
this fluid—
wet part of my self.

Swimming

Other-worldly,
full-body immersion,
timed breathing,
breath held,

the flags,
lane lines
and lane markers on the pool bottom—
a cross close to the wall
so I don't forget to tuck, roll and turn,
touch toes to the hard surface.

All is a muted wave—
the flow,
the pace,
dismissal of pain,
pushing every last bodily part
to touch the wall
on some distant-future, shaved date,
just a little
faster than ever before.

The days,
the seconds,
the yards,
dark hours training,
others wearing the water cocoon,
help me think
I am not crazy
while swimming,

:falling:

especially on a long-distance set
when the pace is just right.

There is a groove—
perhaps it's just brain opioids—
although it feels like arrival.

:falling:

Kenosis

Heart a white cascading mountain stream
cold and inviting, teeming with hidden life
unseen source
  flowing, flowing! I cannot know the origin
of forever fullness.

Mind an early June field on a rolling hill
unplowed, allowed to seed and re-seed
growing wild with wispy wheatgrass,
tendrils of golden straw, occasional tiny
purple wild iris
  blooming, blooming! I cannot predict
  full expression, return to seed.

Body full of blood-red sap
pulsating, sensing, consuming and
excreting, ill when at ease, comfortable in disease
  alive, alive! I cannot know
  what exhales every mineral
  seen as animal, plant, human, galaxy.

dancing and spinning and floating,
flying, sowing, owning and releasing.
I empty all of myself out
  What joy! What joy!
  Everything will
  be refilled to overflowing.

:falling:

:deeper:

Deeper

Untethered,
scared, alone on
the moment's edge,
too high for my liking.

No matter how deep,
there is always
deeper.

Potential

I am ready to listen to my patient's cancer:
bone-dry reserves, scattered brain, runaway mind,

shunned by friends, tomorrow's plans,
questions for which I have no answer—the gift

the addiction of imposing my own will
upon uncertainty thrown away,

a backyard compost pile slowly becoming flowers.
I open like an old friend—

familiar laugh, heart first—
holding the unknown.

Group

He attends our truth group,
the cancer pushing him into
frantic search for a noisy cure.

He cuddles up to the suffering of strangers,
becomes just another tree in the forest
sharing sun, wind, and soil.

He listens,
not too close to be invasive.
Compassionate thoughts of fixing
do not metastasize like kudzu
to steal the light,
choke out the life
they try to shore up.
He sits,
not too far away to abandon.
Fear cannot deter
hesitant roots from connecting
in shared terrain.

His soul stretches toward the sky
as he touches the buried pains,
the finest underground tendrils of another,
and courageously dives deeper;
his waxy leaves brush tenderly
near to others in the unseen breeze.

Front Line

It jars him awake
at 2 a.m., the weight
of a thin silk sheet
on his cheek—
no personal protective equipment
to shield exposure from particles
in the night air.

At 4:15 a.m., she bolts
ahead to make morning rounds,
standing greater than 6 feet apart,
wonders if patient satisfaction scores
will be a tick lower for accessibility.

She tries to calculate how long
her 6-year-old can safely hold
her alcohol-rub, chapped hand
or if she needs to skip
a visit to her diabetic mother out of
an abundance of caution.

He is not accustomed to patients
who ask him to stay safe,
take care of himself,
inquire, *How are you?,*
making it hard to quiet visions
of the young Chinese doctor
on the front line who died.

Above a toilet in the men's room,
a Hippocratic oath sign
proclaims: *I swear to fulfill this*
covenant, to know when I know
not, practice the art.

Tonight they sleep
and dream in color
of virtual meetings
projecting mysterious, indecipherable symbols,
and they pray hard
they will not have to be the one
who decides
who lives,
who dies.

:deeper:

Prayer

You whose name I do not know,
who cannot be known,
eternal exhaler of all things,
I want to whisper something
so softly that only you can hear
with my lips right next
to the tiny hairs on your lower earlobe.

Isolation

Cough droplets flap
butterfly wings, travel
from Wuhan to my rural, American
hometown, sink my
401(k) while doctors in Italy
try to decide whether to use
the last ventilator on a 40-year-old
with 2 kids or a 60-year-old
with hypertension.

We lose all of our saved-up airline money
cancel the trip to Florence
for the wife's 50th birthday, drive to
Sam's Club instead where the toilet paper
is sold out and there, by the entrance,
is a bent-over, homeless man
with a sign PLEASE ANYTHING WILL HELP.

The CDC says to maintain
6 feet of distance,
David Whyte says, *Go to
ground, hold the uncomfortable*. Others
write to make the most of
it all, be mindful of our shared
existence. Politicians jockey to
get elected no matter what.

I light a fire indoors with the help
of a propane igniter, retrieve more wood
from under the covered porch, smell the
smoke from aged, red-oak mix.
From my leather chair, through the window,

:deeper:

I spot the season's first three white cherry blossoms
speckling the gray-brown tree
in this morning's cold, steady,
spring rain.

You sleep in this Sunday morning, well
past the hour when living room lamps automatically
turn off for the day, then awaken, refreshed.

We hug a long drawn-out hug.
I kiss your warm forehead, your
soft cheek and neck,
breathe in your
out breath.

Ode to the Pulp Mill

Great brick-and-stack creator, you stand by a river,
perch on a ridge overlooking the valley.

Massive, rusty-spiked, metal trucks
serve as your emissaries,
feed in 30-year-old, long-leaf pines,
and mulch remnants from the trucks
highlight the shoulders of highways.

Unseen inner workings
transform tree to pulp.
Formaldehydes and ammonia flow
into the river; solvents clean the final product;
fine particulates from combustion
seed the earth in all directions the wind can carry.

Smoke
verifies the presence of a fire within.
Massive plumes rise 24 hours a day.
Clouds balloon upwards for a little distance,
eclipse the mountains behind,
then settle to blanket the whole valley
in pungent, odorous, gray afterbirth.

It brings no comfort to read
that 85 percent of Earth's biomass is plant material,
mostly wood,
 a very small percentage lost during production,
about the same relative amount
as the .01 percent of Earth's living organisms
that are human.

:deeper:

I see you throughout the day
as my patients arrive for radiation treatment,
cough up gray, pale phlegm,
ask how a person who had never smoked
can get lung cancer.

I open
small, medium, and large-size boxes
that hold
necessities and gifts,
desires and guilty pleasures.
Sometimes I see uncomfortable infomercials
where people use your cardboard for their primary residence.

It is now day 17 of the shelter-in-place order,
and the horizon is clean, sky nothing but bright blue,
your furnaces cold.
We order takeout from a nearby restaurant
to support the local economy
and carry it home in the thinnest, colorful box.

:deeper:

This Precious Life

Some say
no one really lives his own life,
true face covered by a mask,

stuck tight and fashioned by a series
of random voices,
interactions,
childhood dreams of flying, long lost,
adult desires for comfort superficially gained,

mismatched pieces welded sequentially over time,
firmly, to the fragile, baby skin
of who we really are.

Some say
all paths lead
to these false lives discarded,
rain-soaked clothes
hanging against
a damp, shadowed stone wall.

Standing here, midlife,
children grown and mostly gone,
I let the cold, winter air in.

Radiant Medicine

On a German battlefield,
just before the bomb hit,
he heard his wife back home whisper,
Go to that ditch over there.

The way he trimmed the beard and hair
of his beloved son's body,
dead from sickle cell,
remembered his usual, parting words
before the ambulance took him away;
If I don't come back this time, remember
you are my hero.

I held my deceased grandmother's
spirit and a lock of her hair
for four seasons,
shared my plate of food every meal,
spoke with her.
A thought finally released:
She could be contained.
The thunder applauded.

Deeper than the electricity
that powers cellular towers,
stronger than constantly pulsating radiation
as microwave generators animate
our individual devices,
broader than the content
of a billion, binged stories:
radiant medicine.

I want to channel it
as your story fills the room,
and tears fog your eyes
to gently cool
your instant, dusk-red cheeks.

It breaks through
at times,
radiant medicine.

acknowledgments

Grateful acknowledgment is made to the editor of the following publication where one of these poems, which has been subsequently revised, originally appeared:

Burningword Literary Journal: "Resurrection"

Thanks to my wife, Laura, for her unwavering support, love, and honesty. Thanks to my parents, Arlene and Peter Mumber, and my sisters, Mary, Lorrie, and Michelle, for allowing me to be myself. Thanks to my friends who helped me explore limits, establish boundaries, and then safely cross them all—especially John Matson, John Pace, Tom Wolfe, Nick Salido, Virginia Swimming 1987 Men's ACC championship brothers, and all of my ROAST family. Thanks to my sons, JT, Samson, and Marcus, for putting up with occasional "Gandhi-dad."

Thanks to my teachers of medicine for nurturing the ability to focus on the whole person—mind, body, heart, and spirit. Dr. Lewis Barnett, Dr. Bernie Siegel, Dr. Andy Weil, and Dr. Rachel Remen inspired me to persist in my dream of being a doctor.

Thanks to my spiritual teachers for showing that what I seek is real. Thich Nhat Hanh, Grandfather Redwolf, Jim Finley, Richard Rohr, and Cynthia Bourgeault showed me that it is okay to be a mistake-laden, unique, ego-based individual *and* follow a unified path of inter-being.

Thanks to all who have worked with Cancer Navigators in supporting its mission that no one has to journey alone, especially in allowing the space for personal transformation. Denise Powers, Kalama Hochreiter, and Heather Reed, as well as countless patients and group members, create the soil that feeds my life and practice.

Thanks to those who helped edit this compilation, including readers like Virginia McChesney, Lee Walburn, and Leigh Schickendantz. Thanks to

Leapfolio, especially Lise Goett for her masterful editing and Jeffrey Levine for his steady guidance. They have helped shape this work in such a way that the reader can have an experience related to the words.

about the author

Matthew Mumber, MD, practices medicine as a board-certified radiation oncologist with the Harbin Clinic in Rome, Georgia. After entering private practice, Matt attended and graduated from Dr. Andrew Weil's fellowship in integrative medicine at the University of Arizona, where he met Rachel Remen and attended trainings on facilitation of physician-patient retreat groups through Commonweal. Subsequently, Matt attended and graduated from a 2-year program on spirituality at the Living School for Action and Contemplation through the Rohr Institute, where he studied with Jim Finley. An author of academic and lay-press texts on the subject of healing, Matt has edited an academic textbook entitled *Integrative Oncology: Principles and Practice* and also co-wrote a lay-press health and wellness book, *Sustainable Wellness*, with Heather Reed. He has served as the president of the Georgia Society of Clinical Oncology.

Matt's poetry, which draws on his personal, professional, cultural, and natural-world experiences, stems from his *lectio divina* meditation and spiritual practice. Matt has facilitated groups and retreats focused on transformation and healing for more than 20 years.

He lives in Georgia with his wife and three sons.

CPSIA information can be obtained
at www.ICGtesting.com
Printed in the USA
JSHW011039260720
6867JS00002B/12